W9-CYV-956

YOU MUST REMEMBER THIS

1979

MILESTONES, MEMORIES,
TRIVIA AND FACTS, NEWS EVENTS,
PROMINENT PERSONALITIES &
SPORTS HIGHLIGHTS OF THE YEAR

TO :

FROM :

MESSAGE :

*selected and researched
by
betsy dexter*

WARNER **W** TREASURES™

PUBLISHED BY WARNER BOOKS

A TIME WARNER COMPANY

Warner Books, Inc.
1271 Avenue of the Americas
New York, New York 10020

Warner Treasures is a
trademark of Warner Books, Inc.

A Time Warner Company

DESIGN:
CAROL BOKUNIEWICZ DESIGN
PRINTED IN SINGAPORE
FIRST PRINTING : MAY 1995
10 9 8 7 6 5 4 3 2 1
ISBN : 0-446-91056-2

Fuel shortages caused many states to impose consumer restrictions. Gasoline sales on odd and even days were instituted across the country.

It was a year when the economy dominated national news—and the news was all bad. The United States inflation rate was 13.3%, the highest it had been in 33 years. Prime interest rates and the foreign trade deficit skyrocketed, as well, and consumption of petroleum products was down 1.8%, the first reduction since 1975. The cost of educating the country's youth went up, but financial hardship and lack of resources sent college enrollment plummeting.

The Shah of Iran was admitted to the United States to undergo surgery, but left for Panama following an uproar over his stay. The U.S. suspended Iranian oil imports and froze Iranian assets in retaliation for the storming of the American embassy in Teheran and the taking of hostages.

On March 28, there was a major accident at **THREE MILE ISLAND,** a nuclear reactor near Middletown, Pennsylvania. As catastrophe loomed, evacuation plans were prepared for people living 10 to 20 miles downwind of the plant. Large antinuclear rallies were held in Washington, DC, and New York City.

JANE M. BYRNE BECAME THE FIRST WOMAN TO BE ELECTED MAYOR OF CHICAGO.

newsreel

patty hearst,

aka Tania, erstwhile Symbionese Liberation Army kidnaping victim, was released from prison on February 1. She served 22 months of a 7-year sentence before being granted clemency by an order from President Carter.

A NEW CABINET-LEVEL DEPARTMENT OF EDUCATION WAS ESTABLISHED, WITH SHIRLEY M. HUFSTEDLER AS ITS FIRST SECRETARY.

'79

IN GREAT BRITAIN, CONSERVATIVE PARTY LEADER **MARGARET THATCHER** BECAME THE FIRST FEMALE PRIME MINISTER.

headlines

international

It was a bad year for United States emissaries abroad. On February 14, the American ambassador to Afghanistan was kidnaped and murdered in Kabul. On November 21, three weeks after the U.S. embassy was overrun in Iran, the U.S. Embassy in Islamabad, Pakistan, was besieged for five hours. Before Pakistani soldiers could restore order, one U.S. marine was killed. On December 2, 11 days later, the U.S. embassy in Tripoli, Libya, was attacked by a mob. Two floors suffered extensive damage, but the 21 people working in the building escaped unharmed.

IN AFGHANISTAN, SOVIET MILITARY FORCES STAGED A MAJOR INVASION AND OVERTHREW THE KABUL GOVERNMENT.

In Uganda, local forces aided by troops from Tanzania liberated their country from the dictatorial clutches of **general idi amin dada**

On February 8, U.S. military ties with Nicaragua were severed and economic aid to the repressive Somoza regime significantly reduced. The American intention was to force Somoza to negotiate with the revolutionary Sandinista movement, which threatened to topple the government. By year's end the guerrillas had captured Managua, and President Somoza had fled.

IN MIDEAST NEWS, AN **EGYPTIAN–ISRAELI PEACE TREATY** ENDED THE 30-YEAR STATE OF WAR BETWEEN THE TWO NATIONS. THE TREATY WAS SIGNED IN A WHITE HOUSE CEREMONY ON MARCH 26 BY SADAT OF EGYPT AND BEGIN OF ISRAEL.

In Vienna, the SALT 2 strategic arms limitation treaty was signed by **Jimmy Carter** and Soviet president **Leonid Brezhnev.**

In Iran, 90 people, including 63 Americans, were taken hostage in the American embassy by militant student followers of the Ayotollah Khomeini. The Ayotollah vowed not to release the U.S. citizens until former shah Mohammad Reza Pahlavi was returned to Teheran to stand trial for his crimes against the Iranian people.

On the art scene, *The Icebergs,* **a painting created by Frederic E. Church in 1861, was auctioned for $2.5 million, the most money ever paid for a painting by an American artist.**

IN TANZANIA, MARY LEAKEY DISCOVERED HUMANLIKE FOOTPRINTS ESTIMATED TO BE 3.6 MILLION YEARS OLD.

A dime-sized silver-and-copper disk found near Bar Harbor, ME, was identified as a Norse coin minted between 1065 and 1080. This marked the first datable Viking artifact found in North America.

bryan allen,

a Californian, made the first man-powered flight across the English Channel. The energetic Allen pedaled a craft 22 miles from the English coast to the French.

THE TERM "ME GENERATION" ENTERED THE AMERICAN VOCABULARY, COURTESY OF SOCIAL CRITIC CHRISTOPHER LASCH'S BOOK ON THE SUBJECT, *THE CULTURE OF NARCISSISM.*

Two of America's favorite pastimes, **smoking cigarettes** and **swilling beer,** were tainted by government reports this year. On the tobacco front, Surgeon General Jules Richmond named cigarette smoking as the single largest environmental factor leading to early death. And in brewski news, researchers announced that trace amounts of nitrosamines, chemicals that may cause cancer, were found in most brands of beer.

home entertainment

AN AM/FM STEREO WITH DOLBY CASSETTE, TURNTABLE, AND TWO SPEAKERS SET THE CONSUMER BACK **$299.**
A 19-INCH COLOR TV WAS **$275.**

cultural
milestones

MEDICAL NOTES

In China, physicians claimed to have constructed a workable hand for a 25-year-old man. The hand, composed of a stainless steel palm covered with grafted muscle and skin, used two toes, transplanted from the recipient's foot, as fingers.

There was great news this year for people who lost parts of their body.

Doctors in Maryland used a metal cylinder to replace an 8-inch section of a woman's spine removed earlier because of cancer.

gadgets

AN ELECTRIC PASTA MAKER WENT FOR **$159.50.**
A CAPPUCCINO MAKER COST **$325.**
A GE FOOD PROCESSOR WAS **$47.99.**

'79

7

This year, it was ABC all the way. The network, which began the decade with but one show in the Top 10, ended it with a whopping 7. The network cast their fortune on a sea of no-brainer sitcoms, most of which either relied on nostalgia: "Laverne & Shirley" and "Happy Days," or innocuous sexual innuendo: "Three's Company," "Mork & Mindy," and "The Ropers."

top-rated tv series of the fall 1979 season:

1. "Laverne & Shirley" (ABC)

2. "Three's Company" (ABC)

3. "Mork & Mindy" (tie) (ABC)

3. "Happy Days" (tie) (ABC)

5. "Angie" (ABC)

6. "60 Minutes" (CBS)

7. "M★A★S★H" (CBS)

8. "The Ropers" (ABC)

9. "All in the Family" (tie) (CBS)

9. "Taxi" (tie) (ABC)

9

'79
milestones

Retired CBS newsman **Eric Sevareid,** 66, and **Susanne St. Pierre,** a 42-year-old producer for "60 Minutes," were married in Worcester, MA, on June 30.

D E A T H S

Conrad Hilton,
founder of the hotel chain that bore his name, died at 91.

Nelson Rockefeller,
four-time governor of New York and vice president from 1974 to 1977, died January 26.

Emmett Kelly,
much-beloved clown, died on March 28 at 80.

Mary Pickford,
one of the first major stars of silent films, died on May 29, at 86.

John Wayne,
the actor who embodied American macho, died of cancer on June 11, at 72.

Arthur Fiedler,
who conducted the Boston Pops Orchestra for 50 years, died on July 10.

James T. Farrell,
two-fisted author of the *Studs Lonigan* trilogy, died on August 22.

Jean Seberg,
actress, died on September 8 at 40.

Elizabeth Bishop,
Pulitzer Prize–winning poet, died on October 6.

Al Capp,
"L'il Abner" creator, died on November 11.

Richard Rodgers,
composer, died on December 30, at 77.

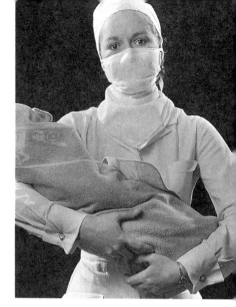

notable birth

KESHIA KNIGHT-PULLIAM, of "The Cosby Show," was born in Newark on April 9.

hit music

1. **my sharona** The Knack
2. **bad girls** Donna Summer
3. **do ya think i'm sexy?** Rod Stewart
4. **reunited** Peaches & Herb
5. **hot stuff** Donna Summer
6. **i will survive** Gloria Gaynor
7. **escape (the pina colada song)** Rupert Holmes
8. **ring my bell** Anita Ward
9. **babe** Styx
10. **too much heaven** The Bee Gees

new wave music, like one-hit wonder The Knack's #1 smash, "My Sharona," was bigger than ever.

ROCK AND ROLL SAW ONE OF ITS MOST FRIGHTENING MOMENTS THIS YEAR WHEN FANS SCRAMBLING TO GET GOOD SEATS FOR A **WHO** CONCERT TRAMPLED 11 PEOPLE TO DEATH AT CINCINNATI'S RIVERFRONT STADIUM.

disco music

was still a big seller on the Top 40 charts. Some of the all-time disco classics hit the airwaves in 1979. Blondie's "Heart of Glass" rang in at #20, and "Y.M.C.A.," by the inimitable Village People, sashayed in at #24.

THIS WAS THE YEAR ELTON JOHN BECAME THE FIRST ROCK STAR FROM THE WEST TO TOUR THE USSR.

bestselling

fiction

1. **the matarese circle**
   robert ludlum

2. **sophie's choice**
   william styron

3. **overload**
   arthur hailey

4. **memories of another day**
   harold robbins

5. **jailbird**
   kurt vonnegut

6. **the dead zone**
   stephen king

7. **the last enchantment**
   mary stewart

8. **the establishment**
   howard fast

9. **the third world war**
   gen. sir john hackett et al.

10. **smiley's people**
    john le carré

THE NOBEL PRIZE FOR
LITERATURE WAS WON BY
ODYSSEUS ELYTIS OF GREECE.

14

books

The boundaries of journalism were redefined this year with the release of new nonfiction by **Tom Wolfe.** Wolfe put his own inimitable stamp on NASA and the astronauts in *The Right Stuff.*

Tom Wolfe

15

IN BASEBALL

it was a year of towering individual accomplishments. St. Louis Cardinal Lou Brock got his 3000th hit. Carl Yastrzemski of the Boston Red Sox hit his 400th major league home run. Pete Rose of the Philadelphia Phillies became the all-time leader in National League singles with 2,427.

THE HIGHEST-PAID ATHLETE IN 1979 WAS BASKETBALL'S MOSES MALONE, WHO EARNED $1 MILLION THIS YEAR.

In an event fraught with geopolitical significance, the Soviet Union's national hockey team defeated the American National Hockey League All-Stars to win the Challenge Cup series.

In college basketball, Michigan State, led by a young super-talent named Magic Johnson, defeated Indiana State 75–64, to win the NCAA championship.

16

Sixteen-year-old
tracey austin
won the women's singles tennis title in Queens, NY, becoming the youngest women's champion in U.S. Open history.

sports

The city of Pittsburgh dominated both baseball and football this year. For the third time, the Pittsburgh Steelers won the Super Bowl, squeaking by the Dallas Cowboys 35–31. Terry Bradshaw of the Steelers was named Most Valuable Player. In baseball, the Pittsburgh Pirates defeated the Baltimore Orioles in one of the most thrilling World Series on record. After 4 games, the Pirates trailed 3 games to 1, but came back to win 3 in a row to cinch the title. Thirty-eight-year-old veteran Willie Stargell was named Most Valuable Player.

The real star of sci-fi epics *Star Trek* and *Alien* were their state-of-the-art special effects. *Alien*'s special effects proved so effective that when the director of photography screened the first clips of the birth sequence, in which a baby alien bursts out of John Hurt's chest, he became ill and had to leave the room.

THE SUCCESS OF SPACE THRILLER *ALIEN* DREW ATTENTION TO HOLLYWOOD'S SWOLLEN PROMOTION BUDGETS. THE FILM COST $11 MILLION TO PRODUCE—BUT THE ADVERTISING CAMPAIGN ADDED $16 MILLION, BRINGING THE FINAL BUDGET TO $27 MILLION.

The big Oscar news this year was **Kramer vs. Kramer.** The domestic divorce drama took Best Picture, Best Actor for **Dustin Hoffman,** Best Supporting Actress for **Meryl Streep,** and Best Director for **Robert Benton.**

top ten box-office stars

1. Burt Reynolds	**6.** Sylvester Stallone
2. Clint Eastwood	**7.** John Travolta
3. Jane Fonda	**8.** Jill Clayburgh
4. Woody Allen	**9.** Roger Moore
5. Barbra Streisand	**10.** Mel Brooks

movies

hit movies

1. *Kramer vs. Kramer* (Columbia)
— $59,986,335

2. *Star Trek—The Motion Picture* (Paramount)
— $56,000,000

3. *The Jerk* (Universal)
— $42,989,656

4. *Rocky II* (United Artists)
— $42,169,387

5. *Alien* (20th Century-Fox)
— $40,300,000

The big news in cars this year came out of Congress. Washington approved a $1.5 billion federal loan guarantee plan for Chrysler Corporation—the largest government bailout of a U.S. company in American history.

cars

Gasohol, a blend of 9 parts unleaded gas with 1 part grain alcohol, was touted as the energy wave of the future. It could be used without modifying a car's carburetor, ignition timing, or fuel lines. It had higher octane, which allowed cars to run with less knocking, improved fuel economy, and lower exhaust emission.

the ford mustang 4

was rated best buy by *Consumer Reports*. The sticker price was $4,187. The Mustang boasted good engine driveability, good normal and emergency handling, effective power brakes, excellent bumper protection, clear instruments, and an effective climate control system with its air conditioner.

Retro and Nostalgia were the big news this year.

fashion

Designers lifted looks from the thirties, forties, and fifties. Padded shoulders, spiked heels, and cocktail chic were everywhere.

Strong bright colors were popular. Reds, chrome yellows, and blues showed up everywhere from scarves and belts to bags and watchbands.

There was a brief sixties revival, most notably in the return of the short skirt. As in the sixties, grosgrain ribbons once again decorated cardigans.

It was the dawn of the Velour Sweatsuit Era. Real trendsetters sported cashmere sweats.

shopping spree

Woman's buttonless cardigan jacket—**$40.**
Woman's pleated baggy pants—**$42.**
For sporty types, Head tennis shorts cost **$36.50.**
Tennis shirts went for **$26.50.**
Sweatsuits were de rigueur, and sold for **$51.**

for the professional woman

6 ounces of Chanel Number 5 cost **$65.**
A preppy short suit cost **$68.**
A legal-sized attaché case cost **$149.50.**
A Coach leather handbag cost **$58.**

quilted fabrics

were huge. The quilted look could be seen on down coats, dinner jackets, at-home pants, and kimonos.

final
factoid

norman mailer transformed the life
and death of Utah's most famous executed mur-
derer, Gary Gilmore, into a towering American
saga in *The Executioner's Song*, which went on
to win the Pulitzer Prize.

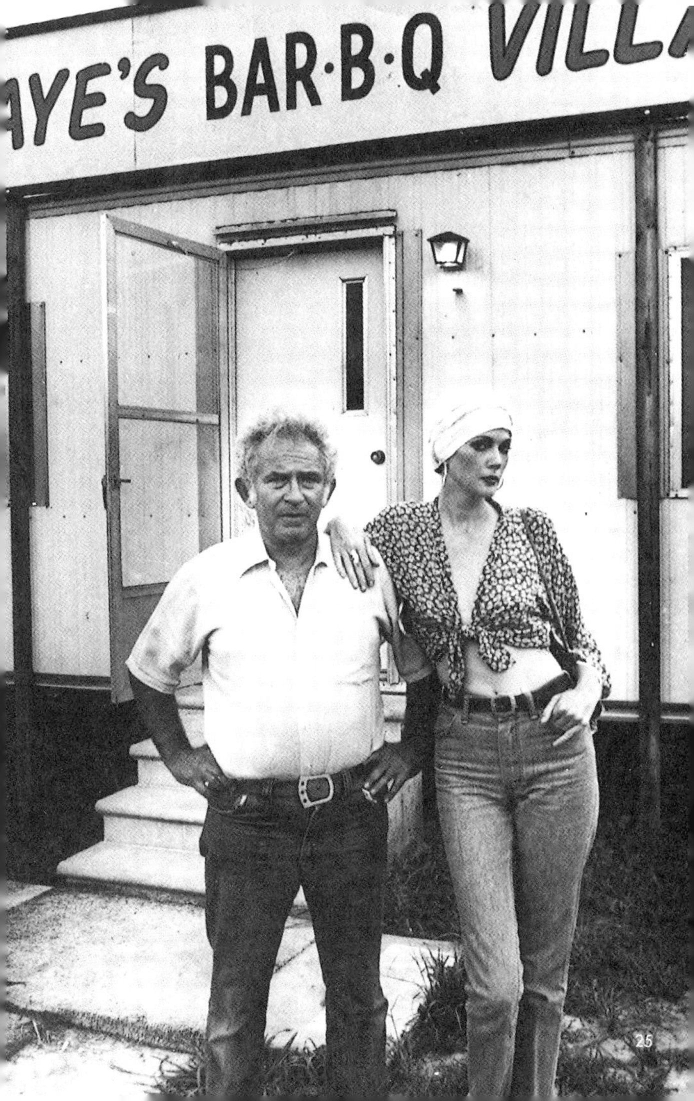
AYE'S BAR·B·Q VILL

archive photos: inside front cover, pages 2, 6, 7,10, 11, 20, 21.

associated press: pages 1, 3, 5, 16, 17, 25, inside back cover.

photofest: pages 9, 15, 18, 19.

original photography:
beth phillips: pages 13, 21, 22.

album cover:
courtesy of bob george/
the archive of contemporary music: page 13

photo research:
alice albert

coordination:
rustyn birch

design:
carol bokuniewicz design
mutsumi hyuga